International Migrants in Johannesburg's Informal Economy

SAMP MIGRATION POLICY SERIES NO. 71

Sally Peberdy

Series Editor: Prof. Jonathan Crush

Southern African Migration Programme (SAMP)
2016

AUTHOR

Sally Peberdy is a Senior Researcher at the Gauteng City-Region Observatory (GCRO), Johannesburg.

ACKNOWLEDGEMENTS

SAMP and ACC would like to acknowledge the financial support of the IDRC for the Growing Informal Cities Project. Dr Paul Okwi of IDRC and Dr Edgard Rodriguez are thanked for their considerable assistance in the implementation of the project. The inputs of Jonathan Crush, Abel Chikanda, Caroline Skinner, David Everatt, Godfrey Tawodzera, Ines Raimundo, Chris Rogerson and Robertson Tengeh are especially acknowledged. Jonathan Crush, Abel Chikanda and Bronwen Dachs assisted with manuscript preparation.

Published by the Southern African Migration Programme, International Migration Research Centre, Balsillie School of International Affairs, Waterloo, Ontario, Canada

First published 2016

ISBN 978-1-920596-18-7

Cover photo by Thom Pierce for the Growing Informal Cities Project

Production by Bronwen Dachs Muller, Cape Town

Printed by Megadigital, Cape Town

CONTENTS

LIST OF TABLES

LIST OF FIGURES

EXECUTIVE SUMMARY

The informal economy plays a significant role in the entrepreneurial landscape of the City of Johannesburg and is patronized by the majority of the city's residents. A 2013 representative survey of Johannesburg residents found that 11% owned businesses of which 65% operated in the informal economy. Despite speculation about the penetration of migrant entrepreneurs in the informal economy, only 20% of informal economy business owners had moved to Gauteng from another country. This means that fully 80% of informal enterprises in Gauteng are South African-owned. Fears about the numbers of international informal economy entrepreneurs and their potential impact on South African businesses are undoubtedly exaggerated but they did escalate in intensity in the 2000s and found expression in violent xenophobic attacks. In Johannesburg, the most recent outbreak of xenophobic violence, including murder and razing of homes and business premises, in January and April 2015. The rhetoric of politicians during and following the xenophobic attacks of 2015 was generally hostile to migrant entrepreneurs.

The policy environment in the city is uneven especially for street traders who operate in the central business district (CBD). In 2013, the City initiated Operation Clean Sweep, which literally swept traders off the street. Although the operation removed all traders regardless of nationality, the municipal re-registration process attempted to limit access to South Africans only. Yet, despite this unwelcoming environment, migrants continue to own and operate businesses in the city.

This paper is based on research conducted by the Growing Informal Cities (GIC) project, a partnership between the Southern African Migration Programme (SAMP), the African Centre for Cities (ACC) at the University of Cape Town, the Gauteng City-Region Observatory (GCRO) and Eduardo Mondlane University in Maputo. A total of 618 interviews were undertaken with migrant and refugee informal economy entrepreneurs in Johannesburg in 2014. Locations for interviews included the CBD, inner-city residential areas, townships and informal settlements. Interviewees were randomly selected using intervals and if they were (a) the owner of the business; (b) not a South African citizen; and (c) their business was not registered for tax and had a turnover of less than ZAR1million per annum. The personal profile of the migrant entrepreneurs was as follows:

- Some 70% were men and 30% were women; 96% were aged between 20 and 49 years; 29% had primary schooling or less, almost 40% had some secondary education, 23% had completed secondary school, and 9% had at least some tertiary education.

- They came from 27 countries of which 21 were in Africa. The majority were born in SADC countries (65%), particularly Zimbabwe (30%) and Mozambique (14%). Some were from Nigeria (7%), the DRC, Lesotho, and Pakistan (5% each), and India (4%).

- At least 46% were asylum seekers, refugees, or permanent residents with permits that allow them to own and operate businesses in South Africa. Another 20% held work permits, mostly Zimbabwean Special Dispensation Permits which again allowed them to operate a business. Another 12% held visitors' permits, while only 12% had no official documentation.

- Less than 5% had arrived in South Africa in 1994 or before. Around 80% had arrived since 2000, with a third arriving between 2000 and 2004, 30% between 2005 and 2009, and 15% between 2010 and 2014.

Migrant entrepreneurs are often perceived to have advantages in business skills and experience compared to South Africans. At the same time, entrepreneurs in the informal economy, regardless of nationality, are often seen as survivalists without entrepreneurial aspirations and skills. As regards these perceptions, the survey found that:

- Over half (56%) of the entrepreneurs had been unemployed before coming to South Africa. However, only 5% were involved in informal entrepreneurial activity and only 2% had owned a business in the formal economy in their home country.

- Almost half (47%) had been unemployed in South Africa before starting their business. Just over a quarter had done semi-skilled or unskilled manual work. However, 5% were professional workers, suggesting that the informal economy offers opportunities not always found in the formal economy.

- Only a minority of the entrepreneurs had prior entrepreneurial experience in South Africa, with 13% having operated a previous informal economy business and 5% owning a business in the formal economy before starting their current business.

- Challenging perceptions that migrant entrepreneurs arrive in South Africa armed with skills that give them advantages over South Africans, 56% said their skills were self-taught, 19% had learned from friends and relatives, and 10% had learned from previous work experience and apprenticeship/on-the-job training. Thirty-seven percent said they did not need any particular skills.

- To assess their entrepreneurial motivations, interviewees were asked to rank a series of factors that had motivated their decision to start their business. Although they felt strongest about the need to increase their financial security, the average score of factors related to survival and financial benefits was lower than factors related to entrepreneurial motivations but higher than the scores related to social capital and altruism and the provision of employment for others.

The survey interviewed migrants in the retail and wholesale (59%), services (30%) and manufacturing (12%) sectors and found the following in relation to their business operations and success:

- For most, there was a considerable time lag between the date of arrival in South Africa and when they started their business. Three-quarters of the businesses were established after 2005 although 55% of respondents had arrived in South Africa before 2005.

- The vast majority (85%) used personal savings as the main source of start-up capital, while 32% also accessed loans from relatives and other individuals. Only 1% had managed to obtain a loan from a bank.

- Amounts of start-up capital were relatively low with 39% having invested less than ZAR5,000, 21% between ZAR5,001 and ZAR10,000, and 19% between ZAR10,001 and ZAR20,000.

- The economy offers opportunities for growth: only 18% still had businesses valued at less than ZAR5,000. Just over half (52%) valued their businesses at over ZAR20,000 even though only 21% had invested more than ZAR20,000 at start-up.

Migrant and refugee entrepreneurs are thought to have a negative economic impact on South Africa and the livelihoods of South Africans. The survey findings challenge these perceptions in a number of ways:

- Migrant entrepreneurs create job opportunities. They had a total of 1,586 employees or 2.6 jobs per business. South Africans held 503 of these jobs (32% of all employees and 41% of all non-family employees).

- Forty-one percent sourced their supplies from formal economy wholesalers, 27% from factories, 17% from supermarkets, and 8% from small shops and retailers. They therefore help create jobs in the formal economy as well as pay VAT.

- Nearly a third (31%) paid rent to a South African company or individual for their business property.

- Migrant entrepreneurs provide goods and services to South Africans in convenient locations and at affordable prices.

Johannesburg provides numerous informal business opportunities but it is also a challenging environment within which to operate a business. Among the problems and challenges most frequently mentioned by the entrepreneurs were:

- The inability to obtain credit from banks for start-up and ongoing investments. Banks cite various reasons for denying credit but a common theme relates to "foreigner" status.

- The police (particularly the Johannesburg Metropolitan Police Department) had a negative impact on their businesses through confiscation, demands for bribes, and physical assault (cited by 19%).

- Entrepreneurs also experience other problems including prejudice because of their nationality (54%), verbal insults against their business (46%), and physical attacks by South Africans (24%). One in five respondents said xenophobia had affected their business operations.

Overall, this report provides insights into the importance of migrant and refugee informal economy entrepreneurial activity to the formal and informal economies of the City of Johannesburg. Instead of trying to sweep the streets clean of these small businesses, the Ministry of Small Business Development, the Gauteng provincial government and the City need to develop policies to grow the SMME economy, develop township economies, and manage the informal economy and street trading. They need to incorporate the businesses owned by migrant entrepreneurs, rather than exclude and demonize them. These businesses make an invaluable contribution to Johannesburg's economy despite operating in a non-enabling political and policy environment.

INTRODUCTION

On 30 September 2013, Johannesburg Mayor Parks Tau launched Operation Clean Sweep, which lasted a month and involved the South African Police Services, the Johannesburg Metropolitan Police Department (JMPD), the Johannesburg Roads Agency, City Power (electricity), Pikitup (rubbish collection and street cleaning), Johannesburg Water, the Metro Trading Company, the national Department of Home Affairs and the South African Revenue Services (customs and excise). It removed traders from the streets, even those who were selling from stands that had been erected by the City and were rented by the traders. Some owners of shops inside buildings were also affected.

According to the Mayor, a reason for the operation was the "need to instil a sense of civic pride and ownership in the inner city."[1] Overall, the operation temporarily removed an estimated 6,000-8,000 traders from the streets of the city, mainly in the CBD. There were also widespread allegations of physical and verbal abuse of migrant and South African informal traders by officials.[2] Although the operation "cleared" all traders regardless of nationality from the streets of the CBD and surrounds, during the re-registration process that was inaugurated to allow some traders to work again, efforts were made by the municipal government – and some traders' associations – to exclude migrant traders.

As Operation Clean Sweep demonstrates, Johannesburg can be a hostile place in which to operate a business as an informal economy migrant entrepreneur. This hostility can emanate from the state but also from competitors, customers and communities. Migrant entrepreneurs operating in the South African informal economy have regularly made media headlines, for all the wrong reasons. Many of these stories tell of shops being looted and destroyed, and of the owners being assaulted and even killed.[3] These incidents have largely involved the residents of the communities where the shops are located. Sometimes the attacks have been led by South African small business associations, including the African Cooperative for Hawkers and Informal Businesses in Johannesburg.

Some traders' associations operating in Johannesburg only allow foreign nationals to be members if they can prove they are legally in the country and have permits that allow them to trade.[4] Other associations are more welcoming and provocations to attack foreign-owned businesses by small business associations do appear to have been more common in Cape Town and other parts of Gauteng than in the City of Johannesburg.[5] However, migrant-owned businesses were again targeted in the xenophobic violence experienced in Soweto and the wider Johannesburg area in January and April 2015.

5

The Gauteng provincial government has indicated that it wants to develop township economies. In his 2014 State of the Province Address, the premier said it is "determined to revitalize and mainstream the township economy by supporting the development of township enterprises, cooperatives and SMMEs that produce goods and services that meet the needs of township residents."[6] The provincial government does not have a formal role in policing the activities of informal entrepreneurs, although its economic policies affect the environment in which they operate. In Johannesburg, the policy of the municipal government towards informal activity has oscillated between accommodation and hostility.[7]

There are good reasons why migrant and refugee entrepreneurs should be included and not excluded from the provincial plan. This argument is based on the evidence of a 2014 survey of migrant entrepreneurs in Johannesburg. The survey was conducted by the IDRC-funded SAMP and ACC Growing Informal Cities (GIC) research project on migrant entrepreneurs in Southern Africa, which in Johannesburg was undertaken with the Gauteng City-Region Observatory (GCRO). The results shed considerable light on how they set up and run their businesses, as well as their economic contribution to the City of Johannesburg.

RESEARCH METHODOLOGY

The GIC research methodology was agreed at collaborative meetings of partner representatives – the Southern African Migration Programme (SAMP), the African Centre for Cities (ACC), Gauteng City-Region Observatory (GCRO), Eduardo Mondlane University (Maputo), and the International Development Research Centre (IDRC). A migrant entrepreneurship survey questionnaire was designed for use in Johannesburg and Cape Town. In Johannesburg, GCRO used a service provider, Quest Research Services, to administer the survey. The interviews were conducted using tablets, which allowed the GPS coordinates of the interviews to be captured. The locations for interviews were selected on the basis of knowledge of the city and where migrant entrepreneurs were likely to be found. Areas chosen included different types of settlements, including the CBD, inner-city residential areas, townships and informal settlements.

A total of 618 interviews were undertaken with international migrant entrepreneurs in Johannesburg in May 2014. The locations of the interviews are shown in Figure 1 and Table 1. A small number of interviews took place just outside the official municipal boundaries of the city but are included in this analysis. Once the location was selected, interviewers used intervals to randomly select interviewees. Potential interviewees were screened by asking if they owned the business, whether they were a South African citizen, and whether the business was in the informal economy. A business was counted as informal if it was not registered for VAT and had a turnover of less than ZAR1 million per annum. The number of employees was not used as a criterion. The survey excluded informal economy entrepreneurs who operated in the transport, mining and finance sectors. Mobile entrepreneurs, home workers, and women migrant entrepreneurs are probably under-represented in this survey as they are more difficult to locate.

Figure 1: Distribution of Respondents in Johannesburg

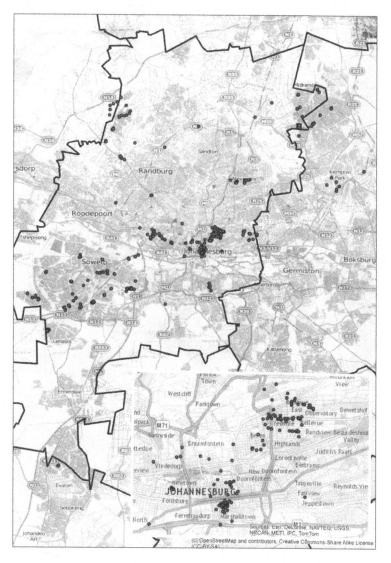

Table 1: Location of Interviews

Location	No.	%
Alexandra	76	12.3
Johannesburg CBD	63	10.2
Baragwanath Hospital	50	8.1
Westbury	47	7.6
Bellevue	42	6.8
Bruma	37	6.0
Yeoville	32	5.2
Rosettenville	31	5.0
Chiawelo	24	3.9
Berea	23	3.7
Hillbrow	23	3.7
Maponya Mall	22	3.6
Lenasia	21	3.4
Ebony Park	19	3.1
Diepkloof	18	2.9
Mayfair	17	2.8
Brixton	13	2.1
Orange Farm	12	1.9
Windsor West	12	1.9
Wynberg	11	1.8
Tembisa	8	1.3
Dobsonville	7	1.1
Kliptown	6	1.0
Protea Glen	2	0.3
Dube	1	0.2
Emdeni	1	0.2
Total	618	100.0

THE INFORMAL ECONOMY

Informal economy entrepreneurship in South African cities encompasses a wide variety of retail, services and manufacturing activity, and ranges across a spectrum from survivalist businesses to enterprises employing relatively large numbers of people.[8] In Johannesburg, retail is easily the most important entrepreneurial activity, involving the sale of a variety of foodstuffs (including sweets, chips, fruit and vegetables, and cooked foods) and items such as clothes and shoes (new, used, and made by the vendor), accessories, cosmetics and other beauty products, books, DVDs and CDs, hardware, electrical goods, soft furnishings, furniture, art and sculptures. Informal entrepreneurs also provide a range of services including hairdressing, fixing and making of shoes and clothes, car repairs and welding. Some technologically-savvy individuals have businesses selling and repairing cell phones and providing computer and internet services. Other informal economy entrepreneurs make and manufacture goods such as metal gates, furniture and arts and crafts, or run construction and artisanal businesses. Geographically, informal businesses can be found on the street and inside (multi-storey) buildings and are also run from residential yards, converted garages, houses, disused factories and old office blocks. They are highly visible at traffic lights, road junctions, mini-bus taxi ranks, alongside the road, and in markets.

A randomized and representative quality of life survey (QoL 2013) of 27,484 Gauteng residents (including 10,042 in Johannesburg) undertaken by GCRO in 2013 found that 11% of the residents of the City of Johannesburg owned their own business and 65% of all business owners operated in the informal economy.[9] Contrary to some commonly held beliefs about the prevalence of cross-border migrant entrepreneurs in the informal economy, only 20% of interviewees who owned businesses in the informal economy in Johannesburg had moved to Gauteng from another country.[10] However, respondents who had moved to Gauteng from another country were more likely to own a business (17%) than those who had moved from another province in South Africa (9%) or had been born in Gauteng (11%). Similarly, business owners in Johannesburg who had moved to Gauteng from another country were more likely to operate in the informal economy (69%) than internal migrants (64%) and the Gauteng-born (63%).[11]

The GCRO QoL 2013 survey interviewed 1,146 business owners in Johannesburg of whom 742 operated in the informal economy and 151 had moved to Gauteng from another country.[12] There were marked differences by race and sex, with 78% of black African, 67%

of coloured, 62% of Indian and 22% of white business owners in Johannesburg operating informally. Only 43% of informal economy business owners in Johannesburg were women, but they were more likely to operate an informal than a formal business (69% of female business owners compared to 62% of male). The QoL 2013 survey also found that 64% of Johannesburg's residents had used the informal economy in the previous year. The most common items or services bought were food (94%), hair salons and barbers (36%), clothes (20%), and tailors, sewing and shoe repairs (21%). The most common reasons given for using informal outlets were "good prices and affordability" (64%) and "convenience" (19%).[13]

As there was no baseline population, this GIC survey sample is not necessarily completely representative of the migrant entrepreneur population of Johannesburg. However, GCRO's 2013 QoL 2013 survey was cross-referenced to provide a guideline as to the possible sex ratio and proportions of different nationalities that might be expected in the city. The survey included a limited number of questions on informal economy business ownership and activity, as well as use of the informal economy, and interprovincial and cross-border trade undertaken by respondents. The QoL 2013 survey itself does not claim to be representative of the population of international migrant entrepreneurs operating businesses in Johannesburg. However, it does capture a representative sample of all migrants and was therefore used for cross-checking. Unlike this survey, QoL 2013 interviewed respondents where they lived and not where they operated their businesses and defined an informal business as one which had less than five employees and was not registered for VAT or other tax. Despite these differences, comparisons are made in this report with data gathered in the QoL 2013 survey where relevant.

PROFILE OF MIGRANT ENTREPRENEURS

The population of migrant entrepreneurs interviewed in this study was relatively diverse (Table 2). Some 70% were men and 30% were women. Similarly, QoL 2013 found that 71% of informal business owners in Johannesburg who had moved to Gauteng from another country were men and 29% were women. The majority of respondents in this survey were black African (82%), while 12% were Indian or Asian, 6% coloured or mixed race, and 1% white.[14] The overwhelming majority (96%) were between 20 and 49 years old. Only one interviewee was under 20 and only three were over 60 years old. The largest cohort (almost one-third) was aged between 35 and 39 years.

Table 2: Demographic Profile of Migrant Entrepreneurs

	No.	%
Sex		
Male	434	70.2
Female	184	29.8
Total	618	100.0
Race		
Black	507	82.0
Indian/Asian	71	11.5
Coloured/Mixed race	34	5.5
White	6	1.0
Total	618	100.0
Age		
19 years and under	1	0.2
20-29 years	132	21.4
30-39 years	302	48.9
40-49 years	159	25.7
50-59 years	21	3.4
60+	3	0.5
Total	618	100.0

In terms of educational attainment, 29% had no schooling or only primary education, suggesting that they might struggle with literacy. However, almost one-third had completed high school or had at least some tertiary education. Two (from Uganda and Zimbabwe) had completed an undergraduate degree. The level of education of the respondents varied by country of origin with Zimbabweans being the most educated (only 15% of the respondents from Zimbabwe lacked any formal education). Furthermore, 22% of the respondents from Nigeria had at least a college diploma, while none of the Lesotho respondents had tertiary qualifications.

The respondents came from 27 countries of which 21 were in Africa (Table 3). The majority were born in SADC countries (65%), particularly Zimbabwe and Mozambique (30% and 14% respectively). Some were from Nigeria (7%), the DRC, Lesotho, and Pakistan (5% each), and India (4%). Reflecting the diversity of the migrant population of Johannesburg, there were also respondents from China, Ethiopia, Malawi, Somalia, and Zambia.

Figure 2: Level of Education of Migrant Entrepreneurs

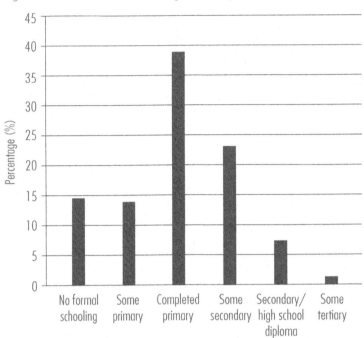

Table 3: Country of Origin of Migrant Entrepreneurs

	No.	%
SADC		
Zimbabwe	186	30.1
Mozambique	89	14.4
DRC	30	4.9
Lesotho	28	4.5
Malawi	20	3.2
Zambia	16	2.6
Swaziland	13	2.1
Angola	11	1.8
Tanzania	7	1.1
East Africa		
Ethiopia	16	2.6
Somalia	16	2.6
Kenya	2	0.3

Eritrea	1	0.2
West Africa		
Nigeria	40	6.5
Cameroon	13	2.1
Ghana	6	1.0
Senegal	1	0.2
Central Africa		
Congo (Brazzaville)	12	1.9
Uganda	12	1.9
Rwanda	6	1.0
North Africa		
Egypt	13	2.1
Asia		
Pakistan	28	4.5
India	23	3.7
China	16	2.6
Bangladesh	11	1.8
Russia	1	0.2
Europe		
France	1	0.2
Total	618	100.0

MOVING TO SOUTH AFRICA

Although racist restrictions on migration to South Africa were lifted in 1986, they remained in force until the 1990s.[15] Refugees were not recognized in legislation until 1998 (a law which only became effective in 2000), but could obtain a form of asylum status from 1993. So, although there were migrants in South Africa before 1994, migration from other African countries (particularly outside SADC), China and South Asia only started in earnest after the demise of apartheid.

The majority of respondents had moved to South Africa after 1994, with the largest cohort – over one-third – arriving between 2000 and 2004, 30% between 2005 and 2009, and a further 15% from 2010 onwards (Figure 3). Interviewees were asked about their immigration status in South Africa (Table 4). While this is a potentially sensitive question, less than 9% of the sample declined to answer. Only 12% said that they had no official documentation allowing them to be in South Africa. At least 46% had permits that definitely allow them to undertake informal entrepreneurial activities in South Africa (permanent residence, refugee and asylum seeker permits).[16] The situation is less clear for the 20% holding work permits as their permits might restrict them to formal sector employment. However, 29% of Zimbabweans said they held work permits. These were probably acquired under the 2010 special dispensation for Zimbabwean migrants.[17] Successful applicants for the dispensation permits are allowed to operate businesses in the informal economy.

Figure 3: Year of Arrival in South Africa

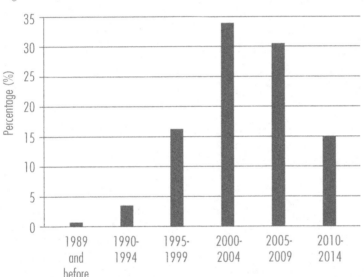

Over half of the respondents (56%) were unemployed in their home countries before moving to South Africa (Table 5). A further 9% had been studying. Among the 21% who had jobs, there were office workers (4%), teachers (2%), employers and managers (1%), and health workers (1%). Other occupations included police/military/security, mine work and agricultural work, gym instruction, making beads and sculptures, traditional medicine, and running households. What this suggests is that very few migrant entrepreneurs in Johannesburg's informal economy had entrepreneurial experience prior to coming to South Africa. Few had gained any business-related experience before their move to South Africa: only 5% were involved in informal entrepreneurial activity and 2% had been self-employed in the formal sector before they left their home country.

Table 4: Immigration Status of Migrant Entrepreneurs

	No.	%
Asylum seeker permit holder	182	29.4
Work permit holder	126	20.4
Visitor's permit holder	74	12.0
No official documentation	72	11.7
Permanent resident of South Africa	55	8.9
Refugee permit holder	45	7.3
Missing/declined to answer	54	8.7
Other	10	1.6
Total	618	100.0

Table 5: Occupations Before and After Coming to South Africa

	Occupation just before leaving home country (%)	Occupations since arriving in South Africa (%)*
Scholar/student	8.7	2.3
Manual worker (unskilled)	7.9	13.5
Manual worker (skilled)	4.9	5.7
Domestic worker	3.7	6.8
Office worker	3.7	2.3
Agricultural worker	1.6	0.8
Teacher	1.6	0.5
Employer/manager	1.0	0.7
Health worker	1.0	0.7
Mine worker	0.8	0.5
Professional	0.7	0.2
Police/military/security	0.5	0.8
Own informal economy business (same activity)	3.7	11.6
Own informal economy business (different activity)	1.0	5.0
Business (self-employed)	2.3	5.0
Other	1.2	2.1
Unemployed/job seeker	55.8	47.4
* multiple response question		

15

Almost half (47%) had been unemployed in South Africa before starting their business (Table 5). Others had found formal employment. Most who had been employed worked as skilled or unskilled manual workers (19%), domestic workers (7%), office workers (2%), in agriculture (1%), and in the security industry (1%). The presence of a few professionals and others who had experience in the formal sector in South Africa suggests that informal entrepreneurship may offer financial and/or other advantages not provided by formal sector employment. Some had prior entrepreneurial experience in South Africa: 12% had operated their own informal economy business doing the same activity and 5% doing a different activity before starting their current business. Another 5% had been self-employed in the formal sector but it is not known in what capacity or sector.

What the respondents intended to do on arrival in South Africa and what they actually did were very different (Table 6). As many as two-thirds said that they had intended to look for a formal sector job. However, many also had entrepreneurial ambitions, with 40% intending to start their own business in South Africa and 12% intending to join a family business. Concern for supporting family members in their home countries was a strong motivation for over 80% of the respondents. Almost half also indicated that they had existing social networks in South Africa, and that they had been encouraged to move by friends and relatives already in the country. The one-third who came as refugees or asylum-seekers were probably more concerned with escaping their home country than with what they would do when they got to South Africa.

Table 6: Intentions on Arrival in South Africa

	Agree (%)	Neither (%)	Disagree (%)
Wanted to provide for my family back home	82	4	14
Intended to look for a formal job in South Africa	67	8	25
Encouraged to come by friends/relatives already in South Africa	48	25	27
Intended to start my own business in South Africa	40	23	38
Came as a refugee/asylum seeker	34	15	51
Intended to join a family business in South Africa	12	17	71
Intended to further my studies in South Africa	9	14	76

BUSINESS OWNERSHIP AND STRATEGIES

DATE OF ESTABLISHMENT

For most entrepreneurs there was a considerable time lag between the date of arrival in South Africa and the date their business was established (Figure 4). Although 17% of the respondents had moved to South Africa between 1995 and 1999, for example, only 4% set up businesses in that period. Similarly, although 34% of the respondents had arrived in South Africa between 2000 and 2004, only 22% of businesses were established in those years. Most had established their current businesses between 2005 and 2009 (35%), or 2010 and 2014 (39%). In part, this may reflect the economic downturn in South Africa in the late 2000s which made it more difficult to find and keep employment. It could also be that respondents were saving money to start their own business as this was the main source of start-up capital.

Figure 4: Comparison between Year of Arrival and Year of Business Establishment

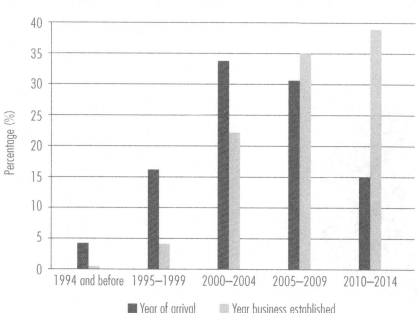

BUSINESS SECTORS

The businesses of migrant entrepreneurs fall into several distinct groups. The main activity (of 59% of the respondents) was in retail and wholesale trade, followed by services (30%), and manufacturing (12%) (Figure 5).[18] The largest cohort of retailers sold food-related products (27% of all entrepreneurs), confectionary (sweets and cakes) (10%) and live animals such as chickens (12%) (Table 7). Other important retail items included clothing and footwear (23%), toiletries and cosmetics (14%), household products (13%) and cigarettes (10%). Many vendors sell more than one product. A typical spaza shop, for example, sells a range of groceries, household goods, toiletries, some fresh fruit and vegetables, and cigarettes and newspapers. Of the 167 respondents in the food trade, 47% sold fresh fruit and vegetables, 29% groceries and 23% cooked food.

Services provided included clothes repair, hair salons and barber shops, photography, laundry, and accommodation. Manufacturing activities included making steel gates, window frames, security doors, and welding as well as furniture making. Others sewed and made arts and crafts, including baskets. Some businesses are involved in more than one sector. For instance, a hair salon owner might include CDs and DVDs among products for sale to clients.

Figure 5: Sector of Participation in the Informal Economy

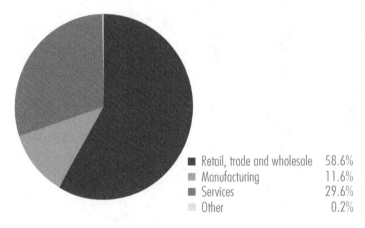

- Retail, trade and wholesale   58.6%
- Manufacturing   11.6%
- Services   29.6%
- Other   0.2%

Table 7: Types of Goods Sold by Migrant Entrepreneurs

	No.	%
All food, including fresh fruit and vegetables and cooked food	168	27.2
Clothing and footwear	139	22.5
Toiletries and cosmetics	86	13.9
Household products	80	12.9
Cigarettes	62	10.0
Confectionary (sweets and cakes)	60	9.7
Accessories (bags, sunglasses etc.)	54	8.7
Arts and crafts (e.g. paintings, beadwork, sculptures)	51	8.3
Electronics	47	7.6
Services	44	7.1
Music/film CDs/DVDs	35	5.7
Sewing/tailoring	32	5.2
Services (haircutting)	30	4.9
Hardware/tools	23	3.7
Newspapers	22	3.6
Livestock (e.g. chickens)	12	1.9
Furniture	10	1.6
Books	5	0.8
Medicine (pharmacy)	5	0.8
Traditional medicine	3	0.5
Other	12	1.9
Note: multiple response question		

START-UP CAPITAL

Most migrants (70%) had started their businesses on their own (Table 8). A minority (16%) had combined with people from their home country and a further 9% with family members to start the business. Only 2% started their business with people from other countries. Connections to South Africans were even weaker, as just 1% had started with local business partners. Consistent with the argument that the informal economy provides opportunities for entry level entrepreneurs and those with low levels of savings, 39% had started their business with ZAR5,000 or less, and 60% with ZAR10,000 or less (Table 9). Some had access to greater amounts of capital with 20% having invested over ZAR20,000. Only 1% had invested over ZAR100,000 in start-up capital.

Table 8: Founder of the Business

	No.	%
I started it alone	434	70.2
I started it with people from my home country	100	16.2
I started it with my family	56	9.1
I started it with people from other countries	13	2.1
I started it with South African business partners	5	0.8
I bought this business from a South African	4	0.6
I bought this business from a non-South African	2	0.3
Other	4	0.8
Total	618	100.0

Table 9: Amount of Capital Used to Start the Business

	Less than ZAR5,000 (%)	ZAR5,001-10,000 (%)	ZAR10,001-20,000 (%)	ZAR20,001-30,000 (%)	ZAR30,001-50,000 (%)	ZAR50,001-100,000 (%)	ZAR100,001-500,000 (%)	N
Gender								
Male	32	20	23	10	10	3	1	413
Female	54	24	13	4	3	2	1	181
Sector								
Retail and wholesale trade	32	22	20	10	11	4	2	351
Manufacturing	31	31	24	7	3	3	0	70
Services	57	15	17	7	4	0	0	172
Total	39	21	19	8	8	3	1	603

Overall, women used less capital to start their businesses than men: over half of the female respondents used ZAR5,000 or less, compared to 32% of men (Table 9). Also, over three-quarters of women used ZAR10,000 or less, compared to 52% of men. Only 14% of the women used ZAR15,000 or more in start-up capital, compared to 35% of men. The services sector appears to require less start-up capital (Table 9). Over half of those in the service sector (57%) had used ZAR5,000 or less to start their business, compared to 32% in the manufacturing sector, and 31% in the retail and wholesale trades. Entrepreneurs in the retail and wholesale trades were most likely to have used more than ZAR15,000 to start their business.

The majority of respondents obtained the capital to start their business from one source, while 23% used two sources, and 3% used three or more. Personal savings were the main source of start-up capital (Table 10). Social networks were important to some with almost one-quarter saying they had obtained a loan from relatives, 8% from other individuals, and 3% from informal financial institutions such as *stokvels* (informal savings groups). Another 3% had used *mashonisa* or money lenders who lend at high (often usurious) rates of interest. Women were marginally less likely than men to have used personal savings and appear to have used social networks (such as *stokvels*) more than men.

Table 10: Sources of Start-up Capital

	Men %	Women %	Total %
Personal savings	86	82	85
Loan from relatives	24	24	24
Loan from non-relatives	8	7	8
Usurers/mashonisa (money lenders)	3	3	3
Loan from informal financial institutions (e.g. stokvels)	1	7	3
Bank loan	2	1	1
Business credit (goods on terms)	0	1	1
Other source	1	1	1
Note: multiple response question			

Very few respondents had accessed formal sources of capital to start their businesses, suggesting a disconnect from the formal financial sector. Less than 10% had applied for a bank loan and 1% had obtained one. Reasons given for why they were rejected included that they were not South African, had incomplete documents, had insufficient guarantees or collateral, their enterprise was not deemed viable, and/or they had insufficient capital. The difficulty of accessing loans from banks was considered a major problem, with interviewees commenting that "it would be better if we could get access to loan money at banks," and that "we need loans so that our businesses can grow." Some suggested that part of the problem was their nationality, saying that there was a "lack of credit facilities because we are foreigners."

Only 7% of the respondents had borrowed money in the previous 12 months to use in their business operations. Again, most relied on informal sources, with 60% having borrowed from family, 25% from usurers/*mashonisas*, and 12% from *stokvels*. Women were twice as likely as men to have borrowed money and were also more likely to have used sources such as *mashonisas* and *stokvels*. Men were more likely to have borrowed from relatives. Very few migrant entrepreneurs had accessed government small business support schemes even though people with permanent residence and refugee status are eligible to apply to some schemes. In total, only 9 respondents (1.5%) had successfully accessed SMME schemes (which were run by the Department of Trade and Industry and the Industrial Development Corporation). All were men. One with ambitions suggested that government should "support foreigners' small businesses so that they can grow into big businesses and provide employment."

BUSINESS SKILLS

Following the outbreaks of xenophobic violence in 2015, the Minister of Small Business Development suggested that migrant informal economy entrepreneurs held "trade secrets" that gave them an unfair advantage over their South African counterparts.[19] The question, then, is where she thinks they learned their business skills, particularly as most had no entrepreneurial experience before coming to South Africa. Over half (56%) said they were self-taught and a further 37% said they did not need any particular skills to run their business (Table 11). Social networks were an important source of skills for one-fifth who had learned from friends and relatives. Previous work experience and apprenticeships had assisted one-tenth of interviewees. Very few had used skills learned in formal training institutions or through non-governmental or governmental training schemes.

Table 11: Source of Skills to Run the Business

	No.	%
Self-taught	346	56.0
No skills needed	231	37.4
Learning from friends and relatives	119	19.3
Previous work experience	39	6.3
Apprenticeship/on the job training	23	3.7
University, school or other training centre	19	3.1
Training courses/programmes (non-governmental including private)	14	2.3
Training courses/programmes (government)	11	1.8
Note: multiple response question		

ENTREPRENEURIAL MOTIVATION

Examining the factors that influence people to start businesses is useful in understanding their entrepreneurial motivation.[20] Broadly, the literature distinguishes between survivalist or necessity-driven entrepreneurs, who are pushed into informal entrepreneurship, and opportunity-driven entrepreneurs, who are pulled into informal entrepreneurship because of the opportunities it provides.[21] The literature leans towards survivalist explanations for starting businesses in the informal economy.[22] These include the need to find a source of income when employment is unavailable or pay is low or uncertain, so that informal entrepreneurship is the only means of financial survival. However, informal economy entrepreneurs may be drawn to start their own businesses for other reasons, including that they feel their personalities are suited to this and their interests lie in the intrinsic rewards it may provide. Some may be encouraged by the social capital that they have, others by altruistic motives, perceived possibilities for social recognition, or upward social mobility.

In South Africa, several studies have begun to explore motivations for entrepreneurship.[23] For instance, a study of 500 informal entrepreneurs in the Gauteng region showed that there were no significant differences between South Africans and immigrants in terms of their motivations to start a business.[24] A study of "necessity entrepreneurs" conducted in Johannesburg showed that women demonstrated stronger entrepreneurial intentions than men.[25] The study argued that women were probably motivated to move from the social position they occupied in the community and starting a business was a way of achieving upward social mobility.

In this survey, interviewees were asked to rank a series of pre-determined factors that might have influenced their decision to start a business on a scale ranging from 1 to 5. The factors were drawn from other studies of the elements that push or draw people into entrepreneurship. A mean score or average weight of each factor was calculated with a score of 5 demonstrating that the factor was extremely important while 1 showed the factor was of no importance in their decision to start their business (Table 12).[26] The responses were grouped into four motivational categories and an average score was calculated for each category.

Table 12 shows that taken individually, some of the reasons classified as financial-survivalist achieved among the highest scores. The strongest motivation of all to start their business was the desire to provide their family with more financial security (mean score of 4.5). This was closely followed by the need to "make more money just to survive" and wanting to "make more money to send to my family in my home country" (both 4.3). However, despite the high rates of unemployment among respondents before starting their businesses, and perhaps because of low expectations of employment conditions, being unemployed (2.5) or in low paid employment (2.2) did not rate highly as motivations (Table 12). The mean score of 3.6 achieved in the financial-survivalist category was not the highest.

On average, respondents identified more strongly with motivations classified as entrepreneurial and related to personal aspirations and intrinsic rewards (mean score 4.1). The survey questions asked the entrepreneurs to indicate the extent to which these, aspirations and identification with personality traits associated with entrepreneurship, motivated them to start their own business. Many were drawn to entrepreneurship because they wanted to be their own boss (4.4), because they like to challenge themselves (4.3), they believe that they have the right personality to run their own business (4.1), they like to learn new skills (4.1) and they wanted to do something new and challenge themselves (4.1). Many also identified relatively strongly with the statements that their risk-taking capacity, competitive nature and desire to run their own business (all 3.9) were important in their decision. The decision to enter informal entrepreneurship can therefore be seen as much more than a survival strategy but rather as a space for meeting entrepreneurial aspirations.

Table 12: Entrepreneurial Motivation

Factor	Mean score
Survivalist/financial benefits and security	
I wanted to give my family greater financial security	4.5
I needed more money just to survive	4.3
I wanted to make more money to send to my family in my home country	4.3
I was unemployed and unable to find a job	2.5
I had a job but it did not pay enough	2.2
Average survivalist/financial	3.6
Entrepreneurial motivations/intrinsic rewards	
I wanted more control over my own time/to be my own boss	4.4
I like to challenge myself	4.3
I have the right personality to run my own business	4.1
I like to learn new skills	4.1
I wanted to do something new and challenging	4.1
I enjoy taking risks	3.9
I wanted to compete with others and be the best	3.9
I have always wanted to run my own business	3.9
Average entrepreneurial/intrinsic rewards	4.1
Social capital/altruism/status	
I wanted to increase my status in the community	3.7
I wanted to contribute to the development of South Africa	3.2
I had a good idea for a service/product to other immigrants	3.0
I wanted to provide a product/service to South Africans	2.9
Support and help in starting my business was available from other immigrants	2.2
My family members have always been involved in business	2.2
I decided to go into business in partnership with others	2.1
Average social capital	2.8
Employment	
I wanted to provide employment for members of my family	2.9
I wanted to provide employment for other people from my home country	2.7
I wanted to provide employment for South Africans	2.1
I had a job but it did not suit my qualifications and experience	1.8
Average employment	2.3

Social capital, altruism and social status have been shown elsewhere to have an important impact on the entrepreneurial motivation of migrants.[27] However, remembering that many respondents started their businesses on their own and without previous experience, such factors were less important than those relating to intrinsic entrepreneurial rewards and financial motivations (Table 12). This category only achieved a mean score of 2.8. The possibility of the informal economy providing opportunities for upward social mobility resonated with some (3.7) (Table 12).[28] In the context of debates around the role of migrant entrepreneurs in South Africa who are often presented as parasitic, it is significant that wanting "to contribute to the development of South Africa" secured a relatively high score (3.2). However, providing employment for others was not a strong motivator to start businesses (at only 2.3)

Overall, men and women showed few differences in their motivations for starting their businesses. Women scored slightly higher on survivalist/financial motivations (mean score of 3.7 compared to 3.5 for men). Women identified more strongly than men with the statements: "I wanted to make more money to send to my family in my home country" (4.7 versus 4.2) and "I had a job but it did not pay enough" (2.4 versus 2.1). There was little difference in male and female identification with entrepreneurial and intrinsic reward motivations (4.0 for women, 4.1 for men). The same was true of motivators related to social capital and altruism. Thus, it seems that in the case of migrant entrepreneurs gender does not make a particularly significant difference to factors influencing decisions to start a business.

BUSINESS PROFITABILITY

One indicator of business success is the current value of the enterprise compared with the capital used to start the business. Here there were many positive signs. Nearly one in five (18%) said their business was worth ZAR5,000 or less (Table 13). However, given that nearly 40% had used ZAR5,000 or less in start-up capital, this suggests a significant improvement for those at the lower end. Around 12% valued their business at ZAR5,001-ZAR10,000, and 18% at ZAR10,001-ZAR20,000. The proportion of those who had businesses valued at over ZAR20,001 had increased from 20% to 43%, and those valued at ZAR50,001 or more from 4% to 21%.

Another indicator used was net monthly profit after expenses (Table 14). Two-thirds (67%) reported net incomes of ZAR5,000 or less per month, and 27% ZAR2,000 or less per month. Monthly net profits of between ZAR5,001 and ZAR10,000 were reported by 19%.

The more profitable enterprises were earning ZAR10,001 to ZAR20,000 per month (10%). The highest profits of over ZAR20,000 were secured by 4%.

Table 13: Current Value of Business and Start-up Capital Used

	Current value (%)	Start-up capital (%)
ZAR5,000 and less	18	39
ZAR5,001–ZAR10,000	12	21
ZAR10,001–ZAR20,000	18	19
ZAR20,001–ZAR30,000	12	8
ZAR30,001–ZAR50,000	10	8
ZAR50,001–ZAR100,000	12	3
ZAR100,001–ZAR500,000	7	1
ZAR500,000 and more	2	0
Don't know	8	2

Table 14: Net Monthly Profit by Sector

	Retail and wholesale (%)	Services (%)	Manufacturing (%)	Total (%)
ZAR500 and less	1.3	8.0	0.0	3.1
ZAR501–ZAR1,000	13.9	18.0	3.6	14.0
ZAR1,001–ZAR2,000	8.6	13.3	9.1	10.0
ZAR2,001–ZA3,000	11.6	18.0	14.5	13.8
ZAR3,001–ZAR4,000	11.6	14.7	23.6	13.8
ZAR4,001–ZAR5,000	12.6	11.3	14.5	12.4
ZAR5,001–ZAR6,000	4.6	6.0	10.9	5.7
ZAR6,001–ZAR7,000	5.6	2.7	10.9	5.5
ZAR7,001–ZAR8,000	4.6	0.7	3.6	3.3
ZAR8,001–ZAR9,000	0.7	2.0	0.0	1.0
ZAR9,001–ZAR10,000	6.3	0.0	1.8	3.9
ZAR10,001–ZAR12,500	3.6	1.3	0.0	2.6
ZAR12,501–ZAR15,000	4.0	2.0	5.5	3.5
ZAR15,001–ZAR20,000	5.0	1.3	0.0	3.3
ZAR20,001 and more	6.0	0.7	1.8	3.9

Profitability clearly varies by sector with services being the least profitable (Table 14). For example, 57% of those in the services sector make profits of ZAR3,000 or less per month compared with 35% of those in retail and 27% of those in manufacturing. Or again, 92% of those in services make ZAR7,000 or less, compared with 87% of those in manufacturing and 69% of those in retail. Most very successful businesses are in the retail sector, with 16% making over ZAR10,000 per month, compared with 7% in manufacturing and 4% in services. While the net monthly profits reported here seem low, they compare relatively favourably with black African incomes in the city (Table 15). Census 2011 found that in Johannesburg, 68% of black African individuals with an income earned ZAR3,200 or less per month compared to 41% of interviewees in this survey.[29] Similarly, the 2013 QoL 2013 survey found that the monthly household income (not individual incomes as in this survey) of nearly two-thirds of black Africans in Gauteng was under ZAR3,200 (Table 15).[30] In this survey 27% of migrant entrepreneurs took home more than ZAR6,401 a month in net profit while only 16% of black African individuals enumerated in Census 2011 had incomes higher than that. Therefore, the informal economy provides migrant entrepreneurs with similar or better incomes than black African individual and household incomes in Johannesburg.

Table 15: Net Monthly Profit Compared to Black African Monthly Incomes, 2011 and 2013

	Net monthly profit migrant entrepreneurs 2014 %	Census 2011 monthly black African individual income (Johannesburg) %	GCRO 2013 monthly black African household income (Johannesburg) %
ZAR3,200 or less	41	68	62
ZAR3,201–ZAR6,400	32	15	21
ZAR6,401–ZAR12,800	16	8	10
ZAR12,801–ZAR25,600	8	5	5
ZAR25,600+	3	3	3

CONTRIBUTING TO THE SOUTH AFRICAN ECONOMY

CONSUMER ACCESS

Where they are able to, entrepreneurs place their businesses where they will find a ready market for their goods or services. Most respondents in this survey ran their businesses from a regular stall or site (Table 16). Almost one-quarter (23%) sold their goods from a permanent stall in a market while almost one in five (18%) sold from a permanent stall on the street/roadside. Others had workshops and used houses, yards and garages. Some used temporary premises that they had to take down every night. Others were more mobile including one who used a caravan and another who was a hairdresser and went to her clients' homes. Nearly 10% had no fixed location and sold goods door-to-door. For South African consumers, migrant entrepreneurs in the informal economy, like their South African counterparts, therefore make consumer goods and foodstuffs more accessible, either geographically or through their pricing strategies.[31] Finding a shaded or sheltered place was a problem for some, with one respondent saying, "there is a problem with the stall because when it's raining we cannot sell anything and we are depending on this business." A hairdresser pointed out the costs of inside and outside premises, saying "when it's raining I will have to work at home or go to a salon where I will have to pay. That makes my profit less."

Table 16: Location of Business Activities

	No.	%
Permanent stall in a market (does not take down stall at night)	153	24.8
Permanent stall on the street/roadside	112	18.1
Temporary stall on the street/roadside (takes down stall at night)	108	17.5
Workshop or shop	96	15.5
Shop in house/yard/garage	65	10.5
No fixed location, mobile (e.g. door-to-door)	48	7.8
In my home	21	3.4
Taxi rank on side of road	17	2.8
Vehicle (car, truck, motorbike, bike)	13	2.1
Taxi/public transport station in permanent structure	3	0.5
In customer's home (e.g. hairstyling)	1	0.2
Other	3	0.5
Note: multiple response question		

RENTING BUSINESS PREMISES

Almost one-third (31%) of the entrepreneurs paid rent to a South African company or individual while a further 12% paid it to the council or municipality (Table 17). Twenty-two percent operated rent free, with or without permission. Those who did not fit any of these categories included 4% who were mobile entrepreneurs, selling door-to-door, as well as from vehicles and at traffic lights. For some, their business premises was also their home. As Table 18 shows, rents varied widely. A quarter (25%) paid less than ZAR500 per month and almost one in five (19%) paid between ZAR500 and ZAR1,000 per month. Those who rented privately from South Africans were proportionally more likely to pay more than ZAR1,000 per month and less likely to pay under ZAR1,000 than those in other occupancy types. One trader commented on the cost of private rentals, saying "we also need shops where we can pay city councils because private owners charge us too much." Another suggested exploitation by South African landlords, saying, "if you are a foreigner South African owners take advantage and charge us too much rent."

Table 17: Tenure/Occupancy Status

	No.	%
Pay rent to private South African owner (company or individual)	194	31.4
I own it/am part owner	127	20.6
Pay rent to council/municipality	72	11.7
Rent-free, without permission (squatting)	71	11.5
Rent-free, with permission	63	10.2
Pay rent to private owner who is not a South African	44	7.1
Door-to-door selling, no fixed location	22	3.6
Share space/premises with others	16	2.6
Pay rent to centre management	6	1.0
Other	3	0.5
Total	618	100.0

Table 18: Amount Paid in Rent per Month

	No.	%
Under ZAR100	4	1.0
ZAR100–ZAR199	15	3.6
ZAR200–ZAR299	26	6.2
ZAR300–ZAR399	47	11.2
ZAR400–ZAR499	13	3.1
ZAR500–ZAR750	36	8.6

ZAR751–ZAR1,000	44	10.5
ZAR1,001–ZAR1,500	43	10.2
ZAR1,501–ZAR2,000	30	7.1
ZAR2,001–ZAR2,500	37	8.8
ZAR2,501–ZAR3,000	35	8.3
ZAR3,001–ZAR3,500	28	6.7
ZAR3,501–ZAR4,000	14	3.3
ZAR4,001–ZAR5,000	26	6.2
ZAR5,001–ZAR6,000	13	3.1
ZAR6,001+	10	2.4
Total	421	100.0

BUYING GOODS AND SUPPLIES

Another way in which South Africans benefit from the activities of migrant entrepreneurs is through their purchasing behaviour. Almost one-third of the entrepreneurs use at least two sources for supplies for their businesses while others use up to five different kinds of outlets. Using all outlets mentioned, 41% of entrepreneurs sourced goods from wholesalers, 27% from factories, 17% from supermarkets, and 8% from small shops and retailers in South Africa (Table 19). A further 11% used fresh produce markets such as the Johannesburg Fresh Produce Market. Only 10% made or grew the goods they sold. All of these outlets, except some of the small retailers and informal markets, should charge VAT. Thus the entrepreneurs not only contribute to the profitability of South African formal sector enterprises and indirectly contribute to job creation in the formal sector, they also contribute to the tax base of the South African economy.[32]

The evidence on whether migrant entrepreneurs combine and engage in bulk purchasing to reduce unit costs is ambiguous. Just over one-third (35%) of the respondents said that they brought goods or supplies for their businesses in bulk together with other business owners (Table 20). Some nationalities were more likely to do so than others. Combined bulk buying was especially common (60% or more of the entrepreneurs) among those from Cameroon, the DRC, Egypt, China, India, Pakistan, and Somalia. With the exception of interviewees from the DRC, SADC nationals were least likely to buy in bulk together (only 23% of Mozambican and 20% of Zimbabwean entrepreneurs). However, strong conclusions should not be drawn from Table 20 given the small numbers involved.

Table 19: Sources of Goods and Supplies for Business

	No.	%
From wholesaler in South Africa	255	41.3
Direct from factory in South Africa	164	26.5
From supermarkets in South Africa	105	17.0
From fresh produce markets in South Africa	68	11.0
Make or grow them themselves	61	9.9
From small shops/retailers in South Africa	51	8.3
From home country	38	6.1
From other informal economy producer/retailer	23	3.7
From another country	21	3.4
Direct from farmers in South Africa	7	1.1
Not applicable	28	4.5
Other	6	1.0
Note: multiple response question		

Table 20: Joint or Group Bulk Purchasing by Migrant Nationality

	No.	%
Pakistan	20	71.4
Congo (Brazzaville)	8	66.7
China	10	62.5
Somalia	10	62.5
Cameroon	8	61.5
Egypt	8	61.5
India	14	60.9
DRC	18	60.0
Ethiopia	9	56.3
Bangladesh	5	45.5
Angola	5	45.5
Malawi	8	40.0
Swaziland	5	38.5
Zambia	6	37.5
Nigeria	11	27.5

Mozambique	20	22.5
Lesotho	6	21.4
Zimbabwe	38	20.4
Ghana	1	16.7
Rwanda	1	16.7
Uganda	2	16.7
Tanzania	1	14.3
Total	215	34.8
Note: multiple response question		

JOB CREATION

The question of whether migrant entrepreneurs take employment opportunities or create them is another contentious issue in policy debates about the role of migrants in the informal economy. In this survey, 263 respondents (43% of all interviewees) employed at least one other person in South Africa. In total they provided 1,586 jobs of which 825 were full-time and 761 were part-time. This amounted to an average of 2.6 jobs per entrepreneur interviewed (618) (Table 21). The employees can be divided into four main types: South Africans, migrants from the same country, migrants from other countries, and family members.

In total these migrant entrepreneurs created 503 full and part-time jobs for South Africans and South Africans constituted 32% of all employees and 41% of all non-family employees. South Africans formed the largest group of part-time employees (35%), outnumbering part-time workers from other countries (30%), family members (18%) and employees from the home countries of interviewees (17%). South Africans made up equal proportions of full-time employees as employees from their home countries and family members (all 28%). Employees from other countries were the smallest category of full-time employees (16%).

In general, migrant entrepreneurs are more likely to employ men rather than women (Table 21). In the part-time category, 66% of the jobs were held by men and only 34% by women. In the full-time category, men occupied 61% of the jobs and women 39%. In every part-time and full-time sub-category, more men were employed than women. This also applied to South African employees. Of the 270 part-time jobs occupied by South Africans, 68% were held by men and 32% by women. With regard to full-time jobs held by South Africans, the ratio was slightly lower (57% men and 43% women). The reasons why migrant entrepreneurs employ more men than women are unclear, but it could be related to factors such as fears about safety and security and (with regard to employment of family members and other migrants) the demography of the migrant population which tends to be male-dominated, or the kinds of work that employees do, some of which might conventionally be performed by men.

Male entrepreneurs (48%) were more likely than women (30%) to employ people in their business while women were less likely than men (10% versus 14%) to employ family members and South Africans (4% and 19% respectively). Entrepreneurs in the retail and wholesale sector were most likely to be employers as almost half (48%) in this sector employed people. This compares to 38% of entrepreneurs in the service sector and 25% engaged in making or manufacturing goods. Ten of the 11 businesses providing car repairs employed people, as did six of eight providing IT and internet services. Other areas where over half of the entrepreneurs employed people included clothing and footwear (57%), haircutting (56%), cooked food (55%), and toiletries and cosmetics (53%).

Table 21: Number, Type and Sex of Employees

	No. of employees	% of total part-time and full-time employees	Average number of employees per employer
Part-time			
South African male employees	183	24.0	3.5
South African female employees	87	11.4	2.1
Sub-total	270	35.4	
Male family members employed	79	10.4	2.1
Female family members employed	55	7.2	1.8
Sub-total	134	17.6	
Male employees from home country	89	11.7	2.2
Female employees from home country	41	5.4	1.4
Sub-total	130	17.1	
Male employees from other countries	152	20.0	2.9
Female employees from other countries	75	9.9	1.7
Sub-total	227	29.9	2.3
Total part-time	761	100.0	

Full-time			
South African male employees	133	16.1	2.5
South African female employees	100	12.1	2.0
Sub-total	233	28.2	
Male family member employed	143	17.3	2.4
Female family members employed	86	10.4	2.2
Sub-total	229	27.7	
Male employees from home country	154	18.7	2.9
Female employees from home country	78	9.5	2.3
Sub-total	232	28.2	
Male employees from other countries	72	8.7	2.6
Female employees from other countries	59	7.2	2.0
Sub-total	131	15.9	2.3
Total full-time	825	100.0	2.4
Total employed	1,586		

MOBILITY AND CROSS-BORDER LINKAGES

OTHER BUSINESSES

There is always a possibility that migrant entrepreneurs' connections to their home countries, or to other countries, enhance their businesses in South Africa or home country. However, only 4% of the respondents (25) said they owned a business outside South Africa with links to their business in South Africa. Fifteen were from Zimbabwe, three each from Pakistan and Mozambique, and one each from the DRC, Ethiopia, Malawi and Nigeria. Twelve were women. Thirteen of these respondents were in retail or wholesale trades, seven manufactured or made their own goods, and five were in the service sector. Over half of this small cohort of migrant entrepreneurs made net monthly profits of ZAR5,000 or less in South Africa, five (20%) had monthly incomes from their businesses of between ZAR5,001-ZAR10,000, and only four (16%) had monthly incomes of over ZAR15,000.

IMPORTS AND EXPORTS

In order to better understand if migrants used their connections to other countries to build their businesses in South Africa, respondents were asked if they imported or exported goods (Table 22).[33] Seventy (or 11% of the total) imported goods from other countries as part of their business. More women imported goods than their male counterparts. Of this cohort, the largest proportion came from neighbouring Zimbabwe and Mozambique. The most common imports included cosmetics, handicrafts and curios, new clothes and shoes, fresh fruit and vegetables, and electronics. A small number imported cell phones and cell phone accessories, CDs and DVDs, textiles, tinned food, rice, mealie meal, fish in some form (fresh, tinned or dried), household goods, and car parts. Imported goods came mainly from Zimbabwe, Mozambique, China, India and Nigeria. Other countries of origin included the DRC, Malawi, Zambia, Angola, Congo-Brazzaville, Egypt, Kenya, Namibia, Tanzania, Ghana, Lesotho, Rwanda, Uganda, Dubai, France, and Japan. Only 13 respondents (2%) exported goods bought in South Africa.

Table 22: Import of Goods to South Africa

	No.	%
Import goods to South Africa		
Yes	70	11.3
No	548	88.7
Import of goods by sex		
Female	40	16.3
Male	30	9.2
Country of origin of those importing goods		
Zimbabwe	20	28.6
Mozambique	10	14.3
China	7	10.0
Nigeria	7	10.0
India	3	4.3
DRC	3	4.3
Other	20	28.6

Goods imported		
Cosmetic/beauty items/hair	13	18.6
New clothes/shoes	13	18.6
Handicrafts/curios	13	18.6
Electronics (DVD players/TVs and stereos)	10	14.3
Fresh/tinned/dried fish	7	10.0
Fresh fruit and vegetables	6	8.6
Cell phone and cell phone accessories	4	5.7
DVDs and CDs	4	5.7
Pre-owned clothes/shoes	4	5.7
Rice/mealie meal	4	5.7
Textiles (capulanas, chitenges)	4	5.7
Tinned/boxed groceries	4	5.7
Household goods (curtains/tablecloths/brooms)	3	4.3
Car parts	1	1.4
Electrical household goods (fridges/cookers/microwaves)	1	1.4
Note: multiple response question		

REMITTANCES

The overwhelming majority of respondents (82%) said one of the reasons for moving to South Africa was to provide for their family back home. For 60%, making more money to send to their family in their home country was very important in influencing their decision to start a business. In practice, almost one-third (31%) had never sent money from their business to people in their home countries, 13% sent money only once a year and 7% less than once a year (Figure 6). Less than 20% are regular remitters, sending money home at least once a month. The remitting behaviour of migrant entrepreneurs in Johannesburg indicates that, although the overwhelming majority had strong intentions of remitting when they arrived in South Africa and set up their businesses, these intentions were not matched by their behaviours. Either their links to home diminish as their businesses grow and they stay longer in South Africa, or their incomes are insufficient to allow them to remit.

Male respondents (36%) were proportionally twice as likely as female (17%) respondents to say that they never sent money to people in their home country. People with no formal schooling (43%) or only primary education (51%) were more likely than those with more education, to say that they never sent money home. There also seemed to be a relationship between migration status and whether respondents sent money home. Thus, 36% of respondents with permanent residence said that they never remitted money, as did 38% of refugees and 29% of asylum seekers. Those with no official documentation were most likely of all not to send money home (39%). Distance also appeared to play a role, with nationals of countries further from South Africa being less likely to send remittances.

Figure 6: Frequency of Remitting to Home Country

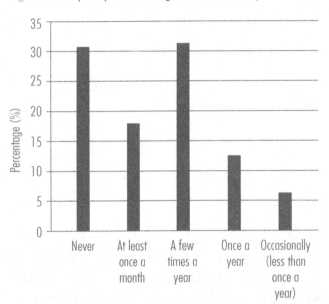

The amounts sent over the previous 12 months varied widely (Table 23). Over half (55%) of the remitters had sent ZAR5,000 or less while one-quarter had remitted between ZAR5,001 and ZAR10,000. One-fifth had sent more than ZAR10,000 in the same period. Respondents were also asked how they sent money home (Figure 7). Some used more than one method with 20% citing two methods and 4% three methods. The majority used informal channels. These included sending it with family, friends or co-workers (27%), using informal money transfers (25%), or taking it themselves (22%). Formal means were used by some with 24% using banks and 23% formal money transfer agencies such as Money Gram or Western Union.

Table 23: Amount of Money Remitted in Previous Year

	No.	%
ZAR1–ZAR1,000	39	10.5
ZAR1,001–ZAR2,000	41	11.1
ZAR2,001–ZAR3,000	33	8.9
ZAR3,001–ZAR4,000	27	7.3
ZAR4,001–ZAR5,000	62	16.8
ZAR5,001–ZAR6,000	27	7.3
ZAR6,001–ZAR7,000	22	5.9
ZAR7,001–ZAR8,000	20	5.4
ZAR8,001–ZAR9,000	5	1.4
ZAR9,001–ZAR10,000	19	5.1
ZAR10,001 and more	75	20.3
Total	370	100.0

Figure 7: Channels for Sending Remittances to Home Country

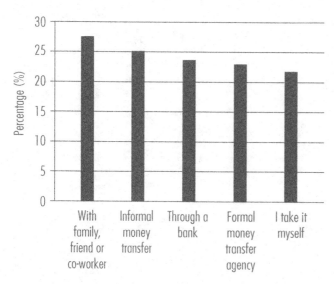

Note: multiple response question

The overwhelming majority of remitters (85%) sent to immediate family members and a further 11% to extended family. Most said that remittances were used for everyday household expenses, including food, school fees, and buying clothes (Table 24). Some used remittances to build, maintain or renovate their dwelling, to buy property, for savings and investments, and for agriculture-related investments. Only 4% were using remittances as savings, sending them to a personal bank account for future use. And just 3% said they had used their remittances to start or run a business, which suggests that remitting is not a major generator of new businesses in the home country of migrants.

Table 24: Use of Remittances

	No.	% of remitters
Buy food	329	76.9
Meet day-to-day household expenses (except food)	160	37.4
Pay educational/school fees	156	36.4
Buy clothes	143	33.4
Pay medical expenses	90	21.0
Build, maintain or renovate their dwelling	84	19.6
For special events, e.g. wedding and funeral expenses	68	15.9
Pay transportation costs	49	11.4
For savings/investment	42	9.8
Buy property	19	4.4
Purchase livestock	18	4.2
For agricultural inputs/equipment	15	3.5
Start or run a business	12	2.8
Note: multiple response question		

BUSINESS CHALLENGES

ECONOMIC AND OTHER PROBLEMS

The business-related problems experienced most often by migrant entrepreneurs were economic in nature and included too many competitors (mentioned by 79% as a frequent or occasional problem), competition from supermarkets and large stores (65%), lack of access to credit (58%), high supplier prices (80%), low sales (89%), and too few customers (90%)

(Table 25). The second group of challenges related to operational details affecting the running of the business. These included a lack of business skills (a concern of 54%), crime and theft (51%), conflict with other entrepreneurs (51%), and storage problems (44%).

Table 25: Problems and Challenges Experienced by Migrant Business Owners

	Often %	Sometimes %
Economic		
Too many competitors around here	30	49
Lack of access to credit	27	31
Competition from supermarkets/large stores	24	41
Suppliers charge too much	23	57
Too few customers	13	77
Customers don't pay their debts	10	30
Insufficient sales	10	79
Operational		
Restricted by lack of training in accounting/marketing/other business skills	13	41
Crime/theft	10	41
Storage problems	8	36
Conflict with other entrepreneurs	4	47
Policing		
Confiscation of goods	8	24
Harassment/demands for bribes by police	8	22
Arrest/detention of self/employees	5	13
Physical attacks/assaults by police	5	14
Discrimination		
Prejudice against my nationality	17	37
Prejudice against my gender	16	23
Verbal insults against my business	13	33
Physical attacks/assaults by South Africans	5	19

Less important proportionally, but by no means insignificant, were the actions of the police, particularly the metropolitan police (JMPD). Problems with the police included confiscation of goods (mentioned by 32%), harassment and demands for bribes (30%), arrest and detention (28%), and physical assault (19%). The economic impact of this abuse was noted by respondents, with one observing that: "Corruption is killing our profit" and another saying: "Metro police must stop abusing people because we depend on our business. That's our living." Another respondent said that the JMPD "always take our stuff and we lose because they take everything from us. I am a breadwinner at home, these days I'm not able to put food on the table because of metros."

Migrant entrepreneurs experienced problems with other people as well. More than half (51%) had experienced some form of conflict with other entrepreneurs and crime/theft. The majority of entrepreneurs said they had experienced prejudice because of their nationality (54%) and verbal insults against their business (46%). Disturbingly, nearly a quarter (24%) said physical attacks by South Africans were often or sometimes a problem for their business. One in five respondents said that xenophobia had affected their business operations either a great deal (13%) or to some extent (7%). Those most affected were from Bangladesh, Pakistan, Ethiopia, Somalia, and Malawi. Only 37% of Ethiopian, 44% of Somali, and 45% of Bangladeshi respondents said their business operations had not been affected by xenophobia. One commented that: "The fact that we are not treated equally, it affects us foreigners." Others were more specific, identifying such problems as "locals threatening to close down my business" and being "assaulted by South Africans because I am a foreigner." Almost four in 10 (39%) complained of gender discrimination.

OPERATION CLEAN SWEEP

In October 2013, the City of Johannesburg undertook what it called Operation Clean Sweep led by the JMPD and the South African Police Services (SAPS), accompanied by officials from the Department of Home Affairs and the South African Revenue Services, as well as arms of the municipal government. The aim of the operation was to clear traders from the streets as well as informal businesses from buildings in certain areas of the city, particularly the central business district. Even traders who had paid rent to the City to sell from stalls erected by the City were forcibly removed. Some shops were also targeted or closed down because of the activity. The media and others recorded traders being beaten, abused and their goods being taken or confiscated. Similar operations were undertaken in other metropolitan and urban areas in Gauteng, including Pretoria (Tshwane) and Hammanskraal (Tshwane). Protesting and resisting traders were shot and killed by police in both Hammanskraal and Pretoria.

The respondents were asked whether they had been affected by Operation Clean Sweep and, if so, what kind of impact it had on their business. Because the interviews with migrant entrepreneurs were undertaken all over Johannesburg and not just in the CBD where Operation Clean Sweep took place, the numbers were not expected to be very high. In total, 10% of the respondents said their businesses had been affected by the operation. Of these, 94% had lost income (Table 26). Just over one-quarter (26%) lost between ZAR1,001-ZAR2,000. Some lost substantial amounts, with one in five losing between ZAR4,001 and ZAR5,000 and one in ten between ZAR5,001 and ZAR7,500. Over half (55%) lost some or all of their stock when their stall or shop was closed down by officials.

Table 26: Financial Cost of Operation Clean Sweep

	No.	%
ZAR500 and less	1	2.0
ZAR501–ZAR1,000	7	14.0
ZAR1,001–ZAR1,500	6	12.0
ZAR1,501–ZAR2,000	7	14.0
ZAR2,001–ZAR3,000	6	12.0
ZAR3,001–ZAR4,000	2	4.0
ZAR4,001–ZAR5,000	10	20.0
ZAR5,001–ZAR7,500	5	10.0
ZAR7,501–ZAR10,000	4	8.0
ZAR10,001 and more	2	4.0

Over half of those affected said that their operations had been shut down with 56% saying they had got their trading space and customers back and 52% that they had their space back but not all of their customers (Table 27). Others had found new trading spaces in the CBD or elsewhere. Many of those who had found a new trading space found it less profitable than their old space. Nearly three-quarters of respondents said they were unable to source goods from their usual sources as their stalls or shops were closed during the operation. Two-thirds had to find new suppliers. Over one-quarter said they were physically assaulted by officials during the operation and almost three-quarters had been verbally abused by officials for being a "foreigner." Overall, the operation was disruptive to people trying to make a livelihood in Johannesburg. The responses of this small cohort of affected entrepreneurs suggest that it was a questionable move by the City and that more careful consideration must be given to how street trading is policed and the attitudes of authorities to migrant entrepreneurs.

Table 27: Impacts of Operation Clean Sweep in Johannesburg

	No.	%
I rely on stock from traders in town and their stalls/shops were closed during the operation	46	72
I was verbally abused by officials for being a foreigner during the operation	46	72
I rely on stock from traders in town and their stalls/shops are still closed so I have had to find new suppliers	42	66
Stall/shop was shut down/removed but I have got my trading space back and my customers	36	56
I lost some or all of my stock when my shop/stall was shut down/removed	35	55
Stall/shop was shut down/removed but I have got my trading space back but have lost customers	33	52
Stall/shop was shut down/removed but I have found a new trading space elsewhere which is less profitable	22	34
I was physically assaulted by officials (e.g. City of Johannesburg/JMPD/police/Home Affairs) during the operation	17	27
Stall/shop was shut down/removed but I have found a new trading space elsewhere which is equally profitable	16	25
Stall/shop was shut down/removed but I have found a new trading space in town which is less profitable	14	22
Stall/shop was shut down/removed but I have found a new trading space in town which is equally profitable	8	13

CONCLUSION

The research presented here provides a rich view of the entrepreneurial activities and enterprises of migrant entrepreneurs in the informal economy of Johannesburg. It is hoped that the information will facilitate understanding of the sector and its potential, and not just in the context of the activities of migrant entrepreneurs. The research challenges many myths or commonly held opinions about foreign migrant entrepreneurs in the City of Johannesburg and shows that they do not dominate the informal economy, which remains largely in the hands of South Africans.[34]

The interviewees came from diverse backgrounds, including a wide range of nationalities, with the overwhelming majority (87%) from the rest of the continent, particularly the SADC. Most of the entrepreneurs interviewed were in the country legally and at least 46% held permits that allowed them to have a business. One in five respondents did not have documents or refused to answer the question. Men comprised the majority of interviewees, reflecting the sex ratio found in migrants from the rest of Africa outside the SADC.

Most interviewees appeared to have chosen to move to South Africa for economic reasons, whether to look for a job, or start a business. However, just over one-third had come as asylum seekers/refugees. Unemployment had been a large part of the lives of some with over half having been unemployed in their home country before moving to South Africa and nearly half having been unemployed in South Africa before starting their business. Over half intended to start a business when they arrived in South Africa (although they may also have considered getting a formal job). That few had previously run a business prior to coming to South Africa challenges the notion that migrant entrepreneurs enter the market with more business skills than South Africans.

Most migrant entrepreneurs operated in the retail and wholesale trades, but nearly one-third provided services and 12% made or manufactured goods. But the entrepreneurial activities of these business owners in the informal economy proved hard to categorize as some operated in more than one sector and sold more than one type of merchandise. Migrant entrepreneurs were found all over the city and selling from a variety of sites. However, lack of appropriate sites that allowed them to store their goods and which protected them, their goods, as well as their customers, from the vagaries of the weather proved to be a problem for a number of interviewees.

Most migrants started their business on their own with less than one-third having relied on social capital through family and other networks to get underway. When asked a series of questions about the factors influencing their decision to start a business, the majority agreed with statements regarding their personality traits which show an entrepreneurial inclination, and their responses to other statements suggest that for most their decisions to start a business were not only based on being unemployed or having inadequate employment. Rather, for the majority, it appears to have been an entrepreneurial decision. However, less than one-quarter could cite specific ways or places that they had learned skills that they used in their business activity and over half said they were self-taught, suggesting that they were not necessarily experienced entrepreneurs prior to starting their business.

Access to capital was a problem for some. For more than half, the amount of capital used to start their business was low as they had used less than ZAR10,000. In part, this may be because most interviewees did not appear to have access to capital other than their own personal savings. However, some did have access to much larger amounts, including the 20% who invested over ZAR20,000. Many rued their inability to access capital through banks or government schemes to either start their business or expand it. However, although many said it was difficult to get a loan from a bank, only 9% had actually applied for a bank loan for start-up capital or for other inputs once their business was established.

The profits ranged widely, with some making as much as ZAR20,000 and more per month. Over two-thirds took home ZAR5,000 or less. However, when the distribution of income is considered against black African incomes (regardless of nationality) in Johannesburg from Census 2011 and GCRO QoL 2013 data, the incomes of these entrepreneurs are often more than commensurate with those of other black Africans. Black African incomes in the province remain low. As several had previously been professionals, and others had been employed, the decision to become a business owner and stay with it suggests that incomes and working conditions (and perhaps the freedom of owning your own business) are better than being in employment.

These entrepreneurs make contributions to the South African economy in a number of ways. In particular, they provide employment. This fact flies in the face of accusations that "foreigners steal jobs." The 263 respondents who employed people in their business provided 1,586 full or part-time jobs, 503 of which were held by South Africans. Second, they contribute to the formal economy when buying goods for their business with the overwhelming majority using the formal sector to source goods and supplies for their businesses. As these outlets should be charging and paying VAT, this means that these migrant entrepreneurs contribute to the government fiscus when they buy goods, even if they do not charge or pay VAT in their own business activities. These findings highlight the complex intersections between the formal and informal sectors and suggest that the value chains of consumer goods in the city are complex. These relationships are extended when the premises used by traders are considered. Almost two-thirds rented their premises. Some (12%) paid rent to the municipality for their stall, while one-third paid rent to South African private sector landlords, whether companies or individuals. Only 11% used rent-free sites without permission and another 20% owned the property they operated their business from. At the same time, they are providing goods and services that are in demand.

Prior to starting the study, it was thought that family and business ties to home countries would be stronger. During the interviews, the respondents suggested that they wanted to maintain strong ties to their home country with more than 80% saying that one of their motivations for coming to South Africa was to provide for their families in their home country, and more than 80% saying that providing for their family in their home country was important to their decision to start a business. However, just over half of respondents never sent money home or did so once a year or less than once a year. It is not clear why this is. Remittances sent to their home countries were largely used for household expenses. Of the 428 respondents who sent remittances, only 8% said it was used to buy property, 7% for savings and investments, and 5% for agricultural inputs, including livestock. Just 3% said they were used to start a business.

Only 4% owned a business outside South Africa. However, just over one in 10 imported goods into South Africa as part of their business and a further 2% exported goods bought in South Africa. With a business in South Africa, imports are more likely than exports. This imbalance between imports and exports suggests that the focus of the entrepreneurial activities of these business owners is in South Africa.

When asked about the problems they faced in running their businesses, they mostly complained about competition and lack of access to capital. Others complained about harsh weather and the lack of appropriate places to sell that would provide protection for them, their goods and customers. Of great concern was the number of traders who said that they had experienced problems with other people. Over half named conflict with other entrepreneurs and crime/theft. Some of this appeared to be xenophobia related with over half saying they had experienced prejudice against their nationality and nearly one-quarter saying that physical attacks by South Africans were often or sometimes a problem for their business. However, when asked directly whether xenophobia had affected their business operations, 70% said "not at all" and 10% "not very much".

Of great concern is the strong narrative of physical and verbal assaults, including xeno-phobic verbal assaults, by the JMPD (metro police) the SAPS, and other officials. Almost one-third said confiscation of goods was a problem, and 30% experienced harassment and demands for bribes by the police. Almost one in five said they experienced physical attacks or assaults by the police. The 67 interviewees who had been affected by Operation Clean Sweep indicated the extent of the problem with 27% saying that they had been physically assaulted by officials (City of Johannesburg/JMPD/SAPS/Home Affairs) during the operation. Another two-thirds had been verbally abused for being a foreigner during the operation.

The xenophobic attitudes of South African competitors, customers, community members and officials may be fed by preconceptions about the activities of cross-border migrant entrepreneurs. This study shows, however, that they make a contribution to the South African economy, through sourcing goods in the formal sector and through paying VAT when they buy goods in the formal sector. Others employ people, including South Africans, and some rent property from South Africans. Better understanding of their contribution may reduce hostility from some quarters. However, the actions of officials, particularly the JMPD, are disturbing. Further research is needed to find out whether the reported physical assaults are related to the nationalities of these entrepreneurs.

Overall, the study has provided insight into these businesses where the profits for many equal or exceed what they might expect to earn if they were in employment. As important, the results of the survey suggest the importance of informal economy entrepreneurial activity to the formal and informal economies of the city. These findings demand much further thought as the Ministry of Small Business Development, the Gauteng provincial government, and the City try to develop policies to grow the SMME sector, develop township economies, and manage the informal economy and street trading.

ENDNOTES

[1] A. Cox, "Claims of Collateral Damage as City Centre gets Massive Clean-Up" *The Star* 24 October, 2013.

[2] M. Nxumalo,"Police Proud of Work around Inner-City 'Clean Up'" *Mail & Guardian* 1 November 2013.

[3] Crush and Ramachandran, *Migrant Entrepreneurship, Collective Violence and Xenophobia in South Africa*.

[4] Manzini and Bénit-Gbaffou, "African Cooperative for Hawkers and Informal Businesses (ACHIB)."

[5] Charman and Piper, "Xenophobia, Criminality and Violent Entrepreneurship"; Gastrow and Amit, *Somalinomics*.

[6] Gauteng Office of the Premier, "State of the Province Address by Premier David Makhura: Thokoza Auditorium, Ekurhuleni Metro" Gauteng Provincial Government, Johannesburg, 2014.

[7] Bénit-Gbaffou, "In Quest for Sustainable Models of Street Trading Management."

[8] Crush et al, *Mean Streets: Migration, Xenophobia and Informality in South Africa*.

[9] S. Peberdy, "Informal Sector Enterprise and Employment in Gauteng" GCRO Data Brief No. 6, GCRO, Johannesburg, 2015.

[10] The term migrant entrepreneur is used in this report when referring to foreign-born entrepreneurs. Entrepreneur is used interchangeably with business owner. Although this study centred on entrepreneurs

operating within the municipal boundaries of the City of Johannesburg, the area is generally referred to as Johannesburg.

[11] Peberdy, "Informal Sector Enterprise and Employment in Gauteng."

[12] Ibid.

[13] Ibid.

[14] Statistics South Africa race classifications were used. This ratio is not unexpected given race ratios in South Africa and among migrants. The QoL 2013 survey found that 78% informal sector business owners were black African, 70% coloured, 57% Indian/Asian and 31% white.

[15] Peberdy, *Selecting Immigrants*.

[16] In August 2015, the South African government proposed changes to the Refugees Act which would restrict asylum seekers from running businesses.

[17] The survey did not specifically ask respondents if they held Zimbabwe these permits

[18] GCRO QoL 2013 found that in Johannesburg 56% of informal sector business owners were in the retail or wholesale trades, 21% provided services, 3% made or manufactured goods and 20% of activities were classified as 'other.'

[19] Minister Lindiwe Zulu in K. Magubane, "Reveal trade secrets, minister tells foreigners" *Business Day*, 28 January 2015.

[20] Carsrud and Brännback, "Entrepreneurial Motivations."

[21] Williams, "Entrepreneurs Operating in the Informal Economy"; Williams, "The Motives of Off-the-Books Entrepreneurs"; Williams and Nadin, "Entrepreneurship and the Informal Economy: An Overview."

[22] Chen, "The Informal Economy"; Heintz and Valodia, "Informality in Africa: A Review"; Skinner, "Street Trade in Africa: A Review."

[23] Shane et al, "Entrepreneurial Motivation"; Mitchell, "Motives of Entrepreneurs"; Fatoki and Patswawairi, "The Motivations and Obstacles to Immigrant Entrepreneurship in South Africa"; Thompson," Risky Business and Geographies of Refugee Capitalism in the Somali Migrant Economy."

[24] Radipere, "An Analysis of Local and Immigrant Entrepreneurs in South Africa's SME Sector."

[25] Lindsay, "Entrepreneurial Intentions of Nascent Entrepreneurs Motivated out of Necessity."

[26] The mean score of each factor was calculated by multiplying the scale number by the number of respondents who had selected that rank (extremely important, important, neither, not important, not important at all). The sum for each rank was then added together and divided by the number of respondents (618) to find the mean score.

[27] Anderson and Platzer, *American Made*; Turkina, and Thai, "Social Capital, Networks, Trust and Immigrant Entrepreneurship."

[28] Lindsay, "Entrepreneurial Intentions of Nascent Entrepreneurs Motivated out of Necessity."

[29] Statistics South Africa, Census 2011, SuperCROSS.

[30] www.gcro.ac.za/qolviewer/

[31] The GCRO QoL 2013 survey found the two most common reasons given for using the informal sector were 'good prices and affordability' (64%) and 'convenience' (19%).

[32] On informal and formal entrepreneurial linkages see Meagher, *Unlocking the Informal Economy*.

[33] The QoL 2013 survey found that 1.2% of all respondents in Gauteng said they or a household member took goods out of Gauteng to sell in another province or country while 1% said they brought goods into Gauteng to sell; Peberdy, "Informal Sector Entrepreneurship."

[34] Peberdy, "Informal Sector Enterprise and Employment in Gauteng."

REFERENCES

1. S. Anderson and M. Platzer, *American Made: The Impacts of Immigrant Entrepreneurs and Professionals on US Competitiveness* (Arlington, VA: National Venture Capital Association, 2006).

2. C. Bénit-Gbaffou, "In Quest for Sustainable Models of Street Trading Management: Lessons for Johannesburg after Operation Clean Sweep" *Technical Report*, CUBES and School of Architecture and Planning. Wits University, Johannesburg.

3. A. Carsrud and M. Brännback, "Entrepreneurial Motivations: What Do We Still Need to Know?" *Journal of Small Business Management* 49(2011): 9-26.

4. A. Charman and L. Piper, "Xenophobia, Criminality and Violent Entrepreneurship: Violence against Somali Shopkeepers in Delft South, Cape Town, South Africa" *South African Review of Sociology* 43: 81-105.

5. M. Chen, "The Informal Economy: Definitions, Theories and Policies" WIEGO Working Paper No. 1, Cambridge, MA and Manchester, UK, 2012.

6. J. Crush, A. Chikanda and C. Skinner (eds.), *Mean Streets: Migration, Xenophobia and Informality in South Africa* (Ottawa, Cape Town and Waterloo: IDRC, ACC and SAMP, 2015).

7. J. Crush and S. Ramachandran, *Migrant Entrepreneurship, Collective Violence and Xenophobia in South Africa* SAMP Migration Policy Series No. 67, Cape Town, 2014.

8. V. Gastrow and R. Amit, *Somalinomics: A Case Study on the Economics of Somali Informal Trade in the Western Cape*, ACMS Research Report, Johannesburg, 2013.

9. J. Heintz and I. Valodia, "Informality in Africa: A Review" WIEGO Working Paper No. 3, Cambridge, MA and Manchester, UK, 2008.

10. W. Lindsay, "Entrepreneurial Intentions of Nascent Entrepreneurs Motivated out of Necessity" In J. Brewer and S. Gibson (Eds.), *Necessity Entrepreneurs: Microenterprise Education and Economic Development* (Cheltenham: Edward Elgar, 2014), pp. 118-144.

11. S. Manzini and C. Bénit-Gbaffou, "African Cooperative for Hawkers and Informal Businesses (ACHIB)" In C. Bénit-Gbaffou (ed.) *A Political Landscape of Street Trader Organisations in Inner City Johannesburg, Post Operation Clean Sweep* (Johannesburg: CUBES and Wits School of Architecture and Planning, 2013), pp. 19-56.

12. K. Meagher, *Unlocking the Informal Economy: A Literature Review of Informal-Formal Economy Linkages in Developing Countries*, WIEGO Working Paper No. 27, (2013), WIEGO: Cambridge, MA and Manchester, UK.

13. B. Mitchell, "Motives of Entrepreneurs: A Case Study of South Africa" *Journal of Entrepreneurship*, 13(2004): 167-183.

14. S. Peberdy, *Selecting Immigrants: National Identity and South Africa's Immigration Policies, 1910-2008* (Johannesburg: Wits University Press, 2009).

15. N. Radipere, "An Analysis of Local and Immigrant Entrepreneurs in South Africa's SME sector" *Mediterranean Journal of Social Sciences* 5(2014): 189-98.

16. S. Shane, E. Locke and C. Collins, "Entrepreneurial Motivation" *Human Resource Management Review* 13(2003): 257-79.

17. O. Fatoki and T. Patswawairi, "The Motivations and Obstacles to Immigrant Entrepreneurship in South Africa" *Journal of Social Sciences* 32(2012): 133-142.

18. C. Skinner, "Street Trade in Africa: A Review" WIEGO Working Paper No. 5, WIEGO: Cambridge, MA and Manchester, UK, 2008.

19. D. Thompson, "Risky Business and Geographies of Refugee Capitalism in the Somali Migrant Economy of Gauteng, South Africa" *Journal of Ethnic and Migration Studies* (2015).

20. E. Turkina, and M. Thai, "Social Capital, Networks, Trust and Immigrant Entrepreneurship: A Cross-Country Analysis" *Journal of Enterprising Communities: People and Places in the Global Economy*, 7(2013): 108-124.

21. C. Williams, "Entrepreneurs Operating in the Informal Economy: Necessity or Opportunity Driven?" *Journal of Small Business and Entrepreneurship* 20: 309-320.

22. C. Williams, "The Motives of Off-the-Books Entrepreneurs: Necessity- or Opportunity-Driven? *International Entrepreneurship and Management Journal* 5: 203-217.

23. C. Williams and S. Nadin, "Entrepreneurship and the Informal Economy: An Overview" *Journal of Developmental Entrepreneurship* 15: 361-378.

MIGRATION POLICY SERIES

1 *Covert Operations: Clandestine Migration, Temporary Work and Immigration Policy in South Africa* (1997) ISBN 1-874864-51-9

2 *Riding the Tiger: Lesotho Miners and Permanent Residence in South Africa* (1997) ISBN 1-874864-52-7

3 *International Migration, Immigrant Entrepreneurs and South Africa's Small Enterprise Economy* (1997) ISBN 1-874864-62-4

4 *Silenced by Nation Building: African Immigrants and Language Policy in the New South Africa* (1998) ISBN 1-874864-64-0

5 *Left Out in the Cold? Housing and Immigration in the New South Africa* (1998) ISBN 1-874864-68-3

6 *Trading Places: Cross-Border Traders and the South African Informal Sector* (1998) ISBN 1-874864-71-3

7 *Challenging Xenophobia: Myth and Realities about Cross-Border Migration in Southern Africa* (1998) ISBN 1-874864-70-5

8 *Sons of Mozambique: Mozambican Miners and Post-Apartheid South Africa* (1998) ISBN 1-874864-78-0

9 *Women on the Move: Gender and Cross-Border Migration to South Africa* (1998) ISBN 1-874864-82-9.

10 *Namibians on South Africa: Attitudes Towards Cross-Border Migration and Immigration Policy* (1998) ISBN 1-874864-84-5.

11 *Building Skills: Cross-Border Migrants and the South African Construction Industry* (1999) ISBN 1-874864-84-5

12 *Immigration & Education: International Students at South African Universities and Technikons* (1999) ISBN 1-874864-89-6

13 *The Lives and Times of African Immigrants in Post-Apartheid South Africa* (1999) ISBN 1-874864-91-8

14 *Still Waiting for the Barbarians: South African Attitudes to Immigrants and Immigration* (1999) ISBN 1-874864-91-8

15 *Undermining Labour: Migrancy and Sub-Contracting in the South African Gold Mining Industry* (1999) ISBN 1-874864-91-8

16 *Borderline Farming: Foreign Migrants in South African Commercial Agriculture* (2000) ISBN 1-874864-97-7

17 *Writing Xenophobia: Immigration and the Press in Post-Apartheid South Africa* (2000) ISBN 1-919798-01-3

18 *Losing Our Minds: Skills Migration and the South African Brain Drain* (2000) ISBN 1-919798-03-x

19 *Botswana: Migration Perspectives and Prospects* (2000) ISBN 1-919798-04-8

20 *The Brain Gain: Skilled Migrants and Immigration Policy in Post-Apartheid South Africa* (2000) ISBN 1-919798-14-5

21 *Cross-Border Raiding and Community Conflict in the Lesotho-South African Border Zone* (2001) ISBN 1-919798-16-1

22 *Immigration, Xenophobia and Human Rights in South Africa* (2001) ISBN 1-919798-30-7

23 *Gender and the Brain Drain from South Africa* (2001) ISBN 1-919798-35-8

24 *Spaces of Vulnerability: Migration and HIV/AIDS in South Africa* (2002) ISBN 1-919798-38-2

25 *Zimbabweans Who Move: Perspectives on International Migration in Zimbabwe* (2002) ISBN 1-919798-40-4

26 *The Border Within: The Future of the Lesotho-South African International Boundary* (2002) ISBN 1-919798-41-2

27 *Mobile Namibia: Migration Trends and Attitudes* (2002) ISBN 1-919798-44-7

28 *Changing Attitudes to Immigration and Refugee Policy in Botswana* (2003) ISBN 1-919798-47-1

29 *The New Brain Drain from Zimbabwe* (2003) ISBN 1-919798-48-X

30 *Regionalizing Xenophobia? Citizen Attitudes to Immigration and Refugee Policy in Southern Africa* (2004) ISBN 1-919798-53-6

31 *Migration, Sexuality and HIV/AIDS in Rural South Africa* (2004) ISBN 1-919798-63-3

32 *Swaziland Moves: Perceptions and Patterns of Modern Migration* (2004) ISBN 1-919798-67-6

33 *HIV/AIDS and Children's Migration in Southern Africa* (2004) ISBN 1-919798-70-6

34 *Medical Leave: The Exodus of Health Professionals from Zimbabwe* (2005) ISBN 1-919798-74-9

35 *Degrees of Uncertainty: Students and the Brain Drain in Southern Africa* (2005) ISBN 1-919798-84-6

36 *Restless Minds: South African Students and the Brain Drain* (2005) ISBN 1-919798-82-X

37 *Understanding Press Coverage of Cross-Border Migration in Southern Africa since 2000* (2005) ISBN 1-919798-91-9

38 *Northern Gateway: Cross-Border Migration Between Namibia and Angola* (2005) ISBN 1-919798-92-7

39 *Early Departures: The Emigration Potential of Zimbabwean Students* (2005) ISBN 1-919798-99-4

40 *Migration and Domestic Workers: Worlds of Work, Health and Mobility in Johannesburg* (2005) ISBN 1-920118-02-0

41 *The Quality of Migration Services Delivery in South Africa* (2005) ISBN 1-920118-03-9

42 *States of Vulnerability: The Future Brain Drain of Talent to South Africa* (2006) ISBN 1-920118-07-1

43 *Migration and Development in Mozambique: Poverty, Inequality and Survival* (2006) ISBN 1-920118-10-1

44 *Migration, Remittances and Development in Southern Africa* (2006) ISBN 1-920118-15-2

45 *Medical Recruiting: The Case of South African Health Care Professionals* (2007) ISBN 1-920118-47-0

46 *Voices From the Margins: Migrant Women's Experiences in Southern Africa* (2007) ISBN 1-920118-50-0

47 *The Haemorrhage of Health Professionals From South Africa: Medical Opinions* (2007) ISBN 978-1-920118-63-1

48 *The Quality of Immigration and Citizenship Services in Namibia* (2008) ISBN 978-1-920118-67-9

49 *Gender, Migration and Remittances in Southern Africa* (2008) ISBN 978-1-920118-70-9

50 *The Perfect Storm: The Realities of Xenophobia in Contemporary South Africa* (2008) ISBN 978-1-920118-71-6

51 *Migrant Remittances and Household Survival in Zimbabwe* (2009) ISBN 978-1-920118-92-1

52 *Migration, Remittances and 'Development' in Lesotho* (2010) ISBN 978-1-920409-26-5

53 *Migration-Induced HIV and AIDS in Rural Mozambique and Swaziland* (2011) ISBN 978-1-920409-49-4

54 *Medical Xenophobia: Zimbabwean Access to Health Services in South Africa* (2011) ISBN 978-1-920409-63-0

55 *The Engagement of the Zimbabwean Medical Diaspora* (2011) ISBN 978-1-920409-64-7

56 *Right to the Classroom: Educational Barriers for Zimbabweans in South Africa* (2011) ISBN 978-1-920409-68-5

57 *Patients Without Borders: Medical Tourism and Medical Migration in Southern Africa* (2012) ISBN 978-1-920409-74-6

58 *The Disengagement of the South African Medical Diaspora* (2012) ISBN 978-1-920596-00-2

59 *The Third Wave: Mixed Migration from Zimbabwe to South Africa* (2012) ISBN 978-1-920596-01-9

60 *Linking Migration, Food Security and Development* (2012) ISBN 978-1-920596-02-6

61 *Unfriendly Neighbours: Contemporary Migration from Zimbabwe to Botswana* (2012) ISBN 978-1-920596-16-3

62 *Heading North: The Zimbabwean Diaspora in Canada* (2012) ISBN 978-1-920596-03-3

63 *Dystopia and Disengagement: Diaspora Attitudes Towards South Africa* (2012) ISBN 978-1-920596-04-0

64 *Soft Targets: Xenophobia, Public Violence and Changing Attitudes to Migrants in South Africa after May 2008* (2013) ISBN 978-1-920596-05-7

65 *Brain Drain and Regain: Migration Behaviour of South African Medical Professionals* (2014) ISBN 978-1-920596-07-1

66 *Xenophobic Violence in South Africa: Denialism, Minimalism, Realism* (2014) ISBN 978-1-920596-08-8

67 *Migrant Entrepreneurship Collective Violence and Xenophobia in South Africa* (2014) ISBN 978-1-920596-09-5

68 *Informal Migrant Entrepreneurship and Inclusive Growth in South Africa, Zimbabwe and Mozambique* (2015) ISBN 978-1-920596-10-1

69 *Calibrating Informal Cross-Border Trade in Southern Africa* (2015) ISBN 978-1-920596-13-2

70 *International Migrants and Refugees in Cape Town's Informal Economy* (2016) ISBN 978-1-920596-15-6

Printed in the United States
By Bookmasters